TOWNS
Down Underground

European badger

Prairie dog

African termites

These animals all build secret towns.

by Gene S. Stuart

Illustrated by James Wilson Harris

BOOKS FOR YOUNG EXPLORERS
NATIONAL GEOGRAPHIC SOCIETY

European Badgers

Evening has come. The sun goes down
while a man and his terrier walk in a meadow.
A little English village grows sleepy.
Underground, a small, secret town
at the edge of a forest is just waking up.

A badger family has slept all day. Now nighttime
is coming. That is a busy time for badgers.
One scratches a tree to mark the family territory.
Another just scratches its ear.
The family looks for things to eat.
Their favorite treat is earthworms.

Cubs play near a hole. This hole is
an entrance that leads down into the town.
Badger towns are called setts.
A sett has tunnels like hallways in a house.
They lead to rooms for sleeping or
to nurseries where cubs are born and raised.

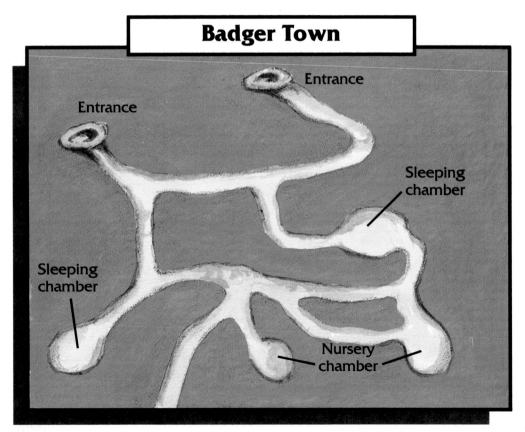

Badger Town

Entrance

Entrance

Sleeping chamber

Sleeping chamber

Nursery chamber

If you could take the top off the ground, like the lid of a pot,
then you would have this bird's-eye view of a badger town.

Badgers tidy the sett.
One found fresh grass
to make a new bed.
It backs down a tunnel
with the grass
tucked under its chin.

Another badger gathers
up an old bed of grass
to throw away.

5

The curious dog smelled badgers.
It follows its nose down a tunnel.
What does it find? Surprise!
A mother badger and her three
tiny cubs are in their nursery.
Badgers are shy, but they can be fierce.
The angry mother drives the terrier away.

Prairie Dogs

Springtime! Prairie dogs pop up from their town.
Some clean each other. Others munch weeds, grass, or
tasty flowers. Pronghorns like to eat weeds, too. Prairie dogs
and pronghorns share the weeds growing near the town.

Look. Listen. What is that? Uh-oh. A truck is coming.
Oh, no! A hawk is flying closer and closer.
A few prairie dogs watch for danger. Their friends feel safe.
They dig new holes, pack dirt down, and find grass for beds.

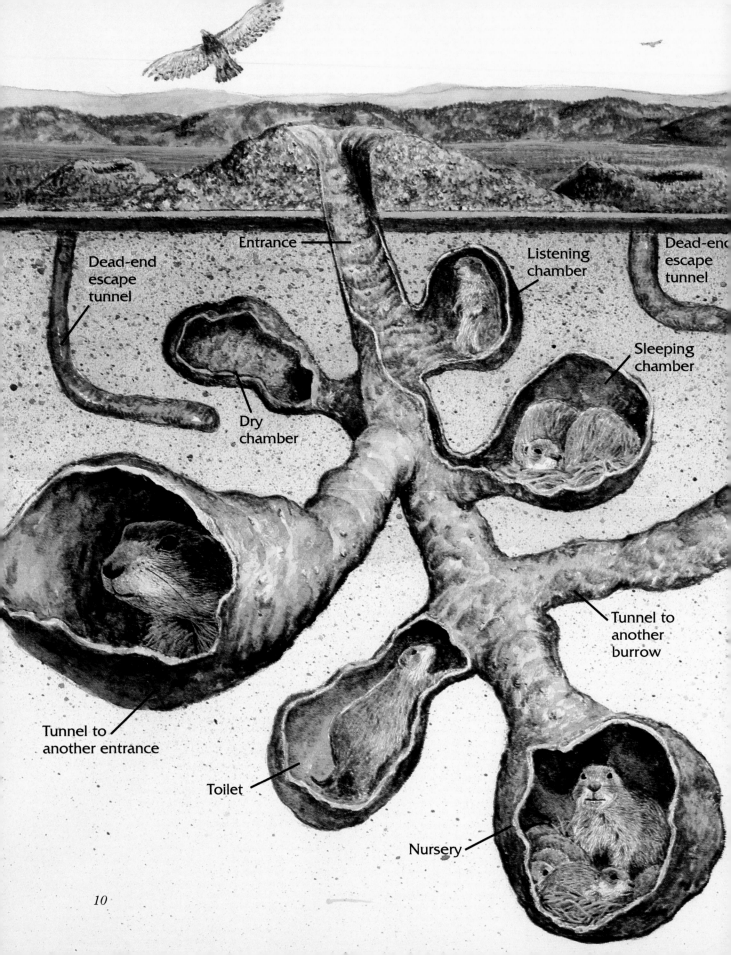

Entrance

Dead-end
escape
tunnel

Listening
chamber

Dead-end
escape
tunnel

Sleeping
chamber

Dry
chamber

Tunnel to
another
burrow

Tunnel to
another entrance

Toilet

Nursery

10

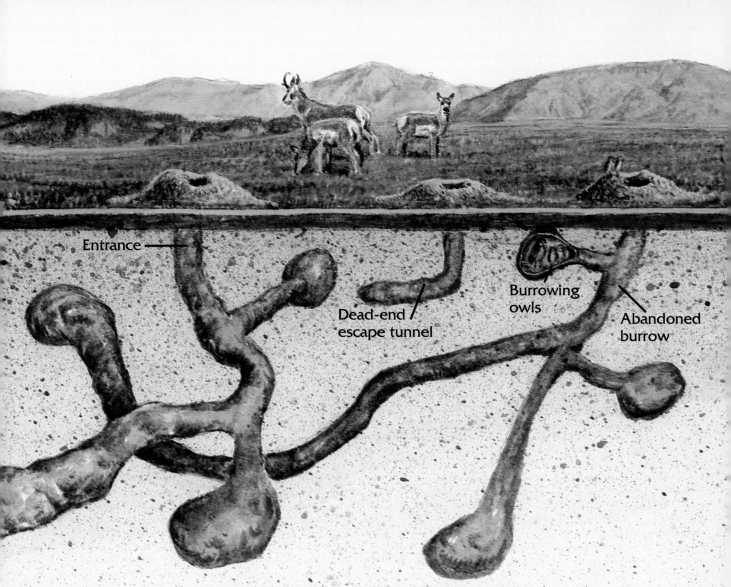

Entrance

Dead-end
escape tunnel

Burrowing
owls

Abandoned
burrow

Prairie Dog Town

Prairie dog towns are like people towns.
Long tunnels are like roads. They lead to neighborhoods.
Each family has a burrow. A burrow is like a house
with different rooms, or chambers. Short tunnels like halls
lead to the chambers. In a chamber near the entrance,
a guard listens for danger. The family goes
to a dry chamber if rain pours into the burrow.
There are sleeping chambers, nurseries, and a toilet.

11

Prairie dogs talk to one another in many ways.
A chirp, a bark, or a whistle says a lot.
A kiss is a big hello to friends and relatives.
Guards on duty send noisy signals above ground,
underground, and all around the town.

Look! An enemy coyote is coming near. A guard
sits up and chirps to say, "Alert!" Another barks,
"Danger! Run down underground." When the coyote
leaves, a guard will whistle, saying, "All clear."

13

When prairie dogs move out,
other animals may move in.
Rabbits find an old burrow.
They also find a little mouse
already living there.

A black-footed ferret comes
prowling through a tunnel.
These animals hunt prairie dogs.
They use old burrows as homes
and as places to raise their young.

Burrowing owls
are good diggers.
But often they nest
in burrows dug
by other animals.
This owl's chicks
have hatched in a
prairie dog town.

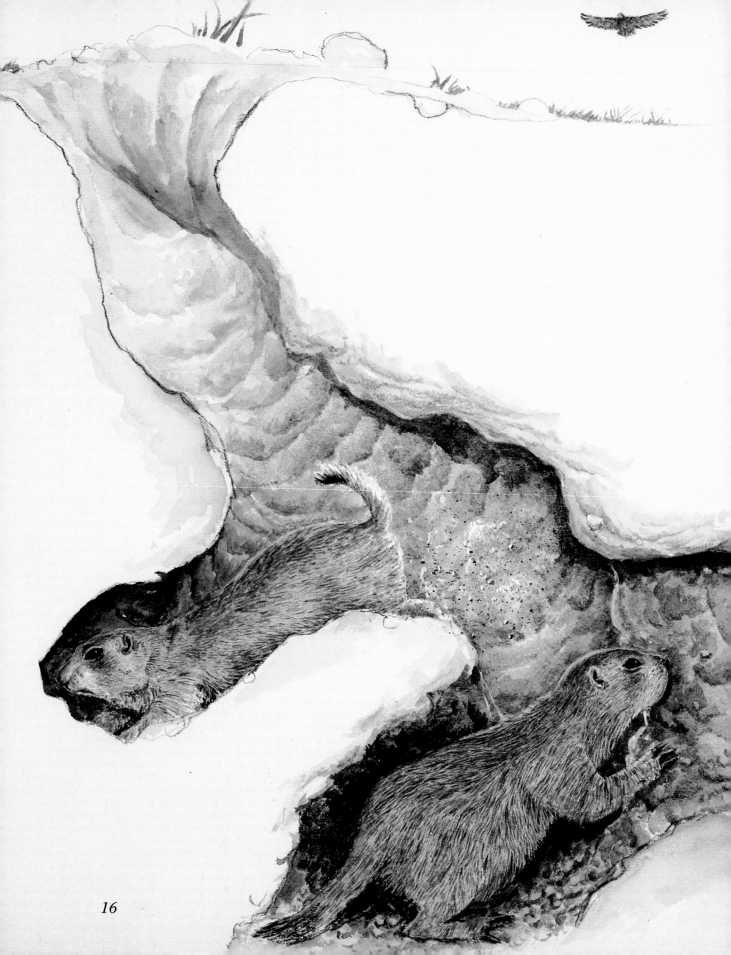

What do prairie dogs do all day? Eat and work. They eat and grow fat for winter. Work helps the burrow, the neighborhood, and the town. They all share chores. They dig burrows and clean rooms. They also take time to play together, just for fun.

A snake has come into the burrow. Hurry! Work fast. While one prairie dog digs, another builds a thick wall to protect the family and its young from the snake.

African Mushroom-growing Termites

Part of this kind of termite town is underground. Part of it rises high above. It is like a big city. Several million of the insects may live here together. The king and queen live in the royal chamber in the center. They never leave it.

Termite Town

Termite mound

Royal chamber

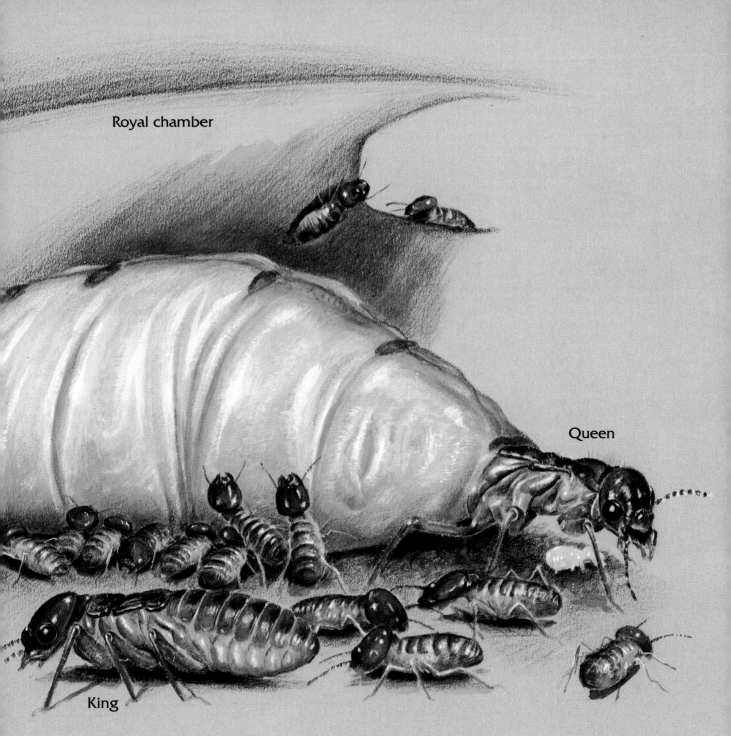

Royal chamber

Queen

King

The queen is the largest termite. She is about the size
of a man's thumb. Every few seconds she lays an egg.
Most babies will become workers or soldiers.
A few will grow up to be queens and kings of new towns.
The most important job in a town is to feed and protect the queen.

19

From the outside, African termite towns look like sand castles. Dwarf mongooses peek out of holes where they live in the sides of a termite mound. Worker termites build the mounds by mixing liquid from their mouths with soil. This makes a kind of cement. Workers also care for the other termites, the eggs, and the babies inside the town. Tiny termite soldiers guard the queen in the royal chamber.

Nursery

Nursery

Nursery

Nursery

The nurseries are the busiest places in town.
Worker termites bring eggs here from the royal chamber
as soon as the queen lays them. Eggs usually hatch
in about three weeks. Workers keep the snow-white
babies clean and fed until they grow into adults.

Workers go outside at night through long tunnels to collect food. Chomp! They bite grass into tiny pieces. They chew these into a mushy mix and spread it on their gardens to help them grow. Garden chambers are above the nurseries.

Mushroom garden

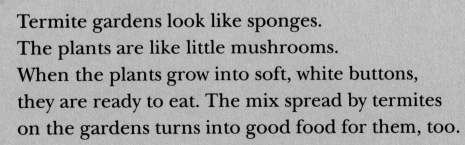

Termite gardens look like sponges.
The plants are like little mushrooms.
When the plants grow into soft, white buttons,
they are ready to eat. The mix spread by termites
on the gardens turns into good food for them, too.

Is it hot outside? Is it cold?
Inside, a termite town stays
just right. Insect body heat
warms the air. When the
air gets hot, it rises. It
cools as it moves down
through tunnels
close to the outside
surface. This air-
conditioning
system keeps
the town the
way termites
like it best.

Termite
mound

Warm air
space

Air tunnels

Mushroom
gardens

Small
air tunnels
where
air cools

Nurseries

Ground level

Royal
chamber

Ground level

Cool air
space

Cool air
space

To water
wells

Termites like the air inside to be damp.
How do they keep it that way? Workers dig wells
under the town. When the air feels dry,
they go down and fill their stomachs with water.
Then they climb back up and spread the water
on the walls. This keeps the air in the rooms damp.

Tiny termites have big enemies that hunt them.
A monitor lizard lies on top of the town.
It lives in a hole in the side and looks for termites.
An aardvark hears termites inside.
It digs into the town with its strong claws.
An aardwolf cannot dig. It licks termites
from the ground with its sticky tongue.

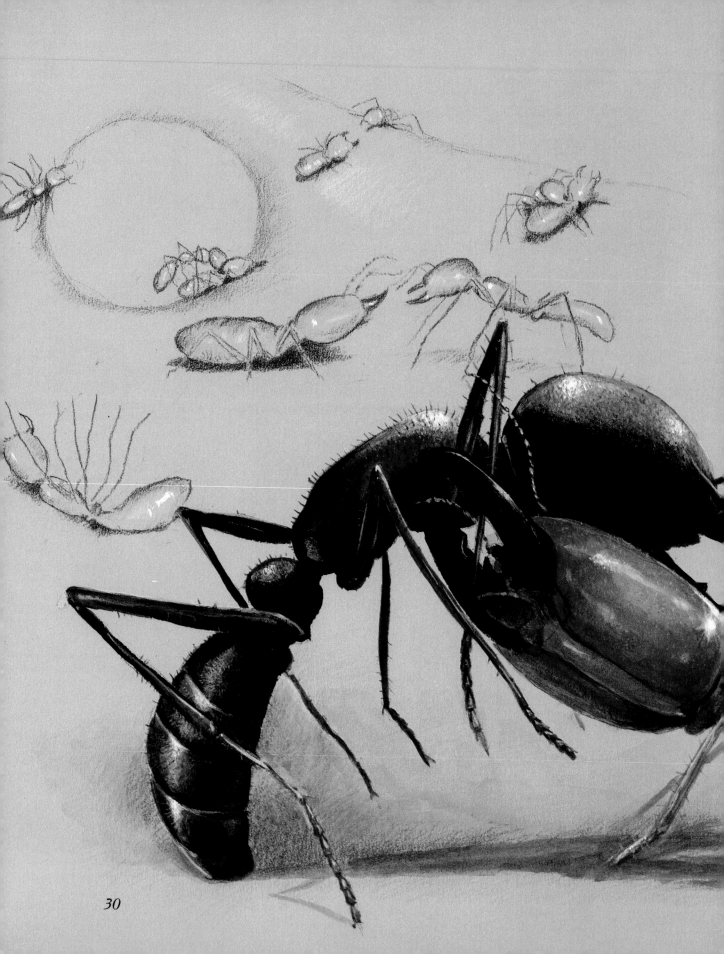

Army ants are some of the termites' worst enemies.
They eat termites and their eggs.
If an aardvark or another animal digs into the town,
an army of black ants may come through the hole.

Army ants are here! A termite soldier sends an alarm.
It beats on a floor or wall with its big, hard head.
Soldiers fight with their sharp mouths.
Workers hurry to build strong walls to keep
the ants out. When enough walls are built,
the queen and the town are safe again.

Published by
The National Geographic Society, Washington, D.C.
Gilbert M. Grosvenor, *President and Chairman
  of the Board*
Michela A. English, *Senior Vice President*
Robert L. Breeden, *Executive Adviser to the President
  for Publications and Educational Media*

Prepared by
The Book Division
William R. Gray, *Director*
Margery G. Dunn, *Senior Editor*

Staff for this book
Jane H. Buxton, *Managing Editor*
Suez B. Kehl, *Art Director*
Elisabeth B. Booz, *Researcher*
Gail N. Hawkins, *Contributing Researcher*
Thomas B. Powell III, *Consulting Illustrations Editor*
Karen F. Edwards, *Design Assistant*
Sandra F. Lotterman, Teresita Cóquia Sison,
  Marilyn J. Williams, *Staff Assistants*

Engraving, Printing, and Product Manufacture
George V. White, *Director,* and Vincent P. Ryan,
  Manager, Manufacturing and Quality Management
Heather Guwang, *Production Project Manager*
Lewis R. Bassford, Richard S. Wain, *Production*

Consultants
Tim W. Clark, Yale University; David H. Kistner, California State
  University; and Ernest G. Neal, Bedford, England,
  Scientific Consultants
Lynda Bush, *Reading Consultant*

Library of Congress CIP Data
Stuart, Gene S.
  Towns Down Underground / by Gene S. Stuart ; illustrated by James Wilson Harris.
    p. cm. — (Books for young explorers)
  Includes bibliographical references.
  Summary: Describes the habitations and ways of life of various animals that live
underground, including the European badger, prairie dog, and African termite.
  ISBN 0-87044-846-3 (regular edition) — ISBN 0-87044-851-X (library edition)
  1. Animals—Habitations—Juvenile literature. 2. Burrowing animals—Juvenile literature.
3. Soil fauna—Juvenile literature. [1. Soil animals. 2. Burrowing animals. 3. Animals—
Habitations.] I. Harris, James Wilson, 1955- ill. II. Title. III. Series.
QL756.S86 1991
591.56'4—dc20   91-19108
                                                                        CIP
                                                                        AC

An African termite town surrounds an acacia tree. The insects chew and recycle dead woody plants. This makes the soil richer and helps plants grow.

Cover: In England, a shy European badger comes out of its hidden home.

MORE ABOUT TOWNS Down Underground

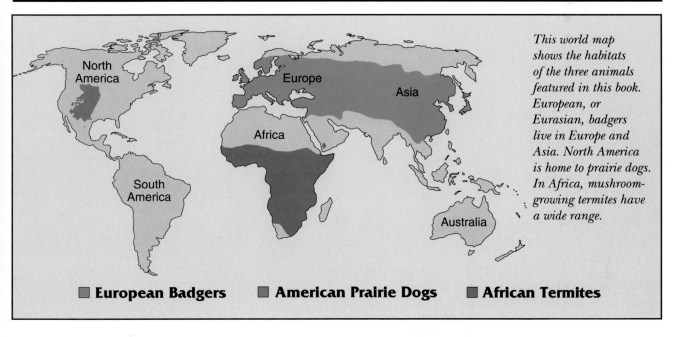

North America

Europe

Asia

Africa

South America

Australia

This world map shows the habitats of the three animals featured in this book. European, or Eurasian, badgers live in Europe and Asia. North America is home to prairie dogs. In Africa, mushroom-growing termites have a wide range.

■ **European Badgers**   ■ **American Prairie Dogs**   ■ **African Termites**

European Badgers

Badgers are mammals that look and walk like little bears, but they are not part of the bear family. They belong to the animal group that includes otters, skunks, weasels, and polecats. These animals all have scent glands at the base of the tail. There are nine badger species in Europe, Asia, Africa, and North America. European, or Eurasian, badgers are among the largest. An adult may be almost a yard long and weigh more than 26 pounds.

These animals live in families, or clans, that may include ten or more animals. Scientists believe that some of their setts are hundreds of years old and have been occupied by many generations of badgers. One group's territory may average 40 acres. Badgers prefer to dig setts in soft, sandy soil near fields and pastures—good areas of food supply.

Badgers are omnivorous. They eat nuts, grains, and fruits, and also insects and weak or dead small animals. Earthworms are one of their favorite foods. A badger can eat several hundred in a few hours. Badgers forage for food, using their strong senses of hearing and smell to search out things to eat as they move along slowly at night.

American Prairie Dogs

Their barking sounds helped give prairie dogs their name, but they are not dogs. These mammals are rodents and belong to the squirrel family. Close relatives are woodchucks and chipmunks. There are five species of prairie dogs. This book features the most sociable kind—black-tailed prairie dogs. These animals live on plains, prairies, and dry grasslands from southern Canada to northern Mexico.

Adult males may weigh three pounds and measure up to seventeen inches. Prairie dogs are herbivores, or plant-eating animals. In summer and autumn, their bodies store fat for winter.

Towns may reach a depth of 12 feet. Neighborhoods are divided into burrows. A family, or coterie, is made up of one or two males and several females and their young. Together they occupy several burrows and escape tunnels.

The number of prairie dogs has decreased by more than 90 percent. A hundred years ago, there were about five billion of them. One prairie dog town in Texas spread over 25,000 square miles and had about 400 million residents.

African Termites

Termites are one of the most ancient kinds of animal still living on earth. They first appeared in the time of dinosaurs, 250 million years ago. Termites are sometimes called white ants, but they are not ants. They are members of the Termitidae family and are also close relatives of cockroaches.

There are about 2,000 different kinds of termites. They are found on every continent except Antarctica. The termites featured in this book inhabit the dry savannas of Africa. All termites live in large groups called colonies. Each colony has a queen and a king that are the parents of all the other termites in the colony.

African fungus-growing termite workers are male or female. They are builders and gardeners, and they feed the king, queen, soldiers, and babies. Soldiers are a little larger, and all of them are female. Soldiers have large heads covered in a kind of armor. Because their mouths are shaped for fighting, they are not able to feed themselves. The workers must put food into the soldiers' mouths. Termites communicate by sounds, vibrations, and information contained in the chemicals in their bodies.

The mature queen is thousands of times heavier than a worker. She may be about four inches long and as big around as a man's thumb. The king is much smaller. It takes the little king about 15 seconds to walk from one end of his wife to the other.

The king and queen live inside the royal chamber and never leave it. Workers constantly groom and feed them. Ordinarily, the queen is the only female in the colony that lays eggs. She produces about 30,000 eggs a day and may live as long as 20 years.

Nobody knows exactly how the insects grow up to be different kinds of termites. All eggs hatch into identical little white nymphs. Most of these grow up to be workers. Some develop further and turn into soldiers. A few become princes and princesses. When there are too few soldiers, more nymphs develop into soldiers to replace them. Or they grow into workers when building needs to be done. How do they know what they should be? It is a mystery.

These African termites live in total darkness inside their enormous clay towns. The busy workers that are master builders and the brave soldiers that defend the town do not have eyes. Their senses of touch and sound help them perform their jobs.

Several nights each year, some young termites become princes and princesses, which have eyes and can see. They will become kings and queens of new towns. At this time they have wings, and they fly out from the town in large swarms. A prince finds a princess, and they find a place for the town. They shed their wings, dig down and build a small room, and seal themselves inside. Neither one will ever need to see again. The new queen begins to lay eggs. Some will develop into workers to feed all the other termites and build the town. Others will grow up to be soldiers to protect it.

When the termites swarm, village people often catch them for food. Roasted, they taste a little like peanut butter. In Kenya and Zimbabwe, men own termite towns and pass them down to their sons.

Additional Reading

Animal Architects. (Washington, D.C., National Geographic Society, 1987). Ages 8-12.

Book of Mammals, 2 vols. (Washington, D.C., National Geographic Society, 1981). Ages 8 and up.

Discovering Badgers, by Martin Banks. (New York, The Bookwright Press, 1988). Ages 6-10.

The Friendly Prairie Dog, by Denise Casey. (New York, Dodd, Mead & Company, 1987). Ages 4-8.

The Insect Societies, by Edward O. Wilson. (Cambridge, MA, Belknap: Harvard University Press, 1971). Reference.

The Insects, by Peter Farb. (Alexandria, VA, Time-Life Books, 1980). Family reference.

Mammals of the National Parks, by Richard G. Van Gelder. (Baltimore, Johns Hopkins University Press, 1982). Reference.

The Natural History of Badgers, by Ernest Neal. (New York, Facts on File, Inc., 1986). Reference.